Helping Children See Jesus

ISBN: 978-1-933206-63-9

ELECTION
*Chosen by God
Old Testament Volume 6
Exodus Part 1*

Author: Arlene Piepgrass
Illustrator: Vernon Henkel
Computer Graphic Artist: Michael Lowery
Typesetting and Layout: Morgan Melton, Patricia Pope

© 2018 Bible Visuals International
PO Box 153, Akron, PA 17501-0153
Phone: (717) 859-1131
www.biblevisuals.org

All rights reserved. No part of this publication may be reproduced, stored in a retrieval system or transmitted in any form by any means, electronic, mechanical, photocopy, recording or otherwise, without the prior permission of the publisher, except as provided by USA copyright law.

RELATED ITEMS

To access related items (such as activities, memory verse posters and translated texts) please visit our web store at shop.biblevisuals.org and enter 2006 in the search box on the page.

FREE TEXT DOWNLOAD

To access a FREE printable copy of the teaching text (PDF format) in English or other available languages, enter S2006DL in the search box. Add the item to your cart, and use coupon code XTACSV17 at checkout. Once your order is processed you will receive an email with a link to the free download.

Ye have not chosen Me, but I have chosen you. John 15:16a

Lesson 1
GOD CHOOSES A NATION

Scripture to be studied: Genesis 12:1-9; 13:15-16; 15:4-5, 13-14; 28:13-15 and all verses in the text.

The *aim* of the lesson: To show that God sovereignly chose Israel as a special nation through which to provide salvation for all the world.

What your students should *know*: That God developed and preserved the nation of Israel for His own purposes.

What your students should *feel*: A willingness to allow God to develop and use their lives for His will.

What your students should *do*:

Saved: Yield themselves to God for His purpose.

Unsaved: Receive the Lord Jesus as their Saviour from sin.

Lesson outline (for the teacher's and students' notebooks):

1. God's purpose in choosing a nation (Genesis 12:1-3).
2. God's promises to this nation (Genesis 13:15-16).
3. God's will concerning the Canaanites (Genesis 15:4-5, 13-14).
4. God works out His plan (Genesis 28:13-15).

The verse to be memorized:

Ye have not chosen Me, but I have chosen you. (John 15:16a)

> **NOTE TO THE TEACHER**
>
> With this volume we begin a study of the wonderful book of Exodus. It is a record of the Israelites leaving their Egyptian bondage and returning to their homeland. Your students will be thrilled to learn of God's ways of choosing (electing) people, things or places for Himself.
>
> "Election is: (1) the sovereign act of God in grace whereby certain persons are chosen from among mankind for Himself (John 15:19); and (2) the sovereign act of God whereby certain elect persons are chosen for distinctive service for Him (Luke 6:13; Acts 9:15; 1 Corinthians 1:27-28)." (*New Scofield Reference Bible* note–1 Peter 5:13.)
>
> Most of the first lesson is actually a review of the book of Genesis. Please keep referring to the map on the back cover so your students will have a geographical understanding of this lesson.

THE LESSON
1. GOD'S PURPOSE IN CHOOSING A NATION
Genesis 12:1-3

Has God ever spoken to you? Suppose He told you that He has chosen you for His special purpose. If He would ask you to leave your homeland, would you do it?

Long, long ago, God talked to a man named Abraham. Abraham lived in the city of Ur. (See Genesis 11:31.) God said, "Abraham, I want you to leave this land. Leave your father and his family and follow Me. I'm going to lead you to a new country. There I will give you many, many descendants." (When parents have children, grandchildren and great-grandchildren, these are their descendants.)

God added, "Abraham, I'm going to give you so many descendants that they will become a great nation." (A nation is a group of people living in the same country, obeying the same laws and having the same leader. *Teacher:* Illustrate from the country in which you live.)

Show Illustration #1

God chose to make a new nation through Abraham for a very special reason. He wanted this nation to be an example to all the nations around them. He wanted other nations to know that God would bless those who love Him, serve Him and worship Him. If this nation obeyed God, they would receive blessings from Him. They would be happy. If they disobeyed God, they would be punished. The other nations would see that the God of this special nation was living, powerful and just. They would understand that people should live to please the true and living God of Heaven. (See Exodus 19:5-6.)

God had still another important reason for making a new nation. He lovingly planned to send His only Son, Jesus Christ, to die for the sins of the whole world. His Son would be born through a young woman chosen from this special nation. (See Genesis 12:3b; 22:18.)

2. GOD'S PROMISES TO THIS NATION
Genesis 13:15-16

When God ordered Abraham to follow Him, He promised, "Abraham, I'm going to make you the father of a great nation. I'm going to give you a land in which to live. I will show you how to live."

God said *He* would do all these things for Abraham. Abraham didn't choose God; God chose Abraham and promised him great blessing. Abraham had to do only one thing: obey God.

So Abraham packed his belongings and said good-bye to his friends. Many doubtless asked, "Abraham, why are you packing everything you own? Where are you going? Why are you leaving? When are you coming back?"

Abraham could only answer, "I don't know where I'll be going. But God, the true and living One, has told me to move. He will show me where to go. I must obey God."

His friends shook their heads sadly. "This man is foolish!" they said. But Abraham didn't care what people said or thought. He had to obey God.

Show Illustration #2

It was a long, hard journey which took many weeks and months. Abraham often stopped. Usually he built an altar. There he prayed to God and offered sacrifices to Him. Finally (after delaying in Haran) Abraham got to Canaan. There God said, "Abraham, this is it! This is the land I will give to you and your descendants." (See Genesis 12:7.)

How happy Abraham was! He saw with his own eyes the land God had chosen especially for him. Immediately he built an altar and worshiped the Lord. (See Genesis 12:8.)

– 19 –

When Abraham and Sarah (his wife) arrived in Canaan, they had no children. Over and over God promised Abraham, "You're going to have many descendants. You're going to be the father of a great nation." (See Genesis 12:2, 7; 13:15-16; 15:4-5.)

Abraham reminded God, "I'm getting older and older, I'm almost 100 years old. Still Sarah and I have no children. But I believe You will do what You have promised."

What Abraham said pleased God. (See Genesis 15:6; Romans 4:3-4, 13-25.) Because of Abraham's faith, God declared him righteous (in right standing with God). Abraham believed God's promise even though he couldn't see how it would take place.

Then one happy day little Isaac was born in the home of Sarah and Abraham. They had trusted God a long time. And God kept His promise. God's special nation was beginning. When Isaac grew up, he married and had twin boys named Jacob and Esau. God showed Isaac that He wanted his son, Jacob, not Esau (the firstborn), to be the father of this nation. Just as God had chosen Abraham, He now chose Jacob.

Do you think God chose Jacob because he was better than Esau? No! God chose Jacob before he was born, before he could do anything good or bad. (See Genesis 25:23; Romans 9:11-13.) Jacob wasn't chosen because he *deserved* to be the father of God's chosen nation. God selected Jacob because this was His divine plan.

God created each of us. He has a right to do with us whatever He chooses. (See Romans 9:11, 20-21.) A man who molds clay pots makes some to hold lovely things. He makes others to hold trash. Likewise, God chooses to use each of us in different ways. He chooses some to be leaders, some to be teachers, some to be helpers.

God is sovereign. That is, He has power over everything. He is in charge. Ever since the beginning, God has had a plan for the world and everyone in it. And He is working out His plan. He has a plan for you and for me. He says to us: "I love you very much. I sent my only Son, Jesus Christ, to die on the cross for your sins. I want you to believe that He died for YOUR sins. I want to use you as I used Abraham, Isaac and Jacob. Will you obey Me? I have a plan for your life." (See John 3:16; Proverbs 3:5-6.)

The promises God had given Abraham, He repeated years later to Jacob. (See Genesis 28:13-15.) God said, "Jacob, I am going to give you many descendants. I'll give you this land to live in. I will never leave you." What wonderful promises!

Jacob's grandparents, Abraham and Sarah, had to wait many long years for Isaac, the one son God had promised them. But God gave Jacob 12 sons. So, you see, God doesn't always work the same way. He has a special plan for each one of us. When our trust is in Him and we obey Him, He works out the one plan which is best for us.

Jacob usually wanted his own way instead of God's way. This often got Jacob into trouble. Nevertheless, God wanted Jacob to believe Him and to obey Him. So one night the Angel of the Lord wrestled with Jacob and touched Jacob's hip. From then on, Jacob was lame.

That same night God said, "Jacob, your name means *trickster*. I am now giving you a new name: Israel. This means *a prince with God*. I will be in charge of your life. I will give you My power."

When the sun came up that morning, Jacob went limping on his way. He would *never* forget that night–the night he saw God face-to-face. And from that time on, Jacob's descendants were called the "children of Israel" or Israelites. (Sometimes today they are called Jews or Israelis.)

3. GOD'S WILL CONCERNING THE CANAANITES
Genesis 15:4-5, 13-14

The Israelites were not the only people who lived in Canaan. Many others who didn't believe in God lived there also. These Canaanites were wicked and served demons. They offered sacrifices to stones and trees because they believed gods lived in them. Some even sacrificed their own children to these false, make-believe gods that could never help them.

Show Illustration #3

God said to the Israelites, "You will be tempted to be good friends with the Canaanites. You'll want to imitate their way of life. Your children will want to marry their sons and daughters. (See Genesis 24:3.) Don't allow it! You may be tempted to worship their idols. Never do so! If you do, I will punish you with judgment and troubles. Be faithful to Me, the true and righteous One."

4. GOD WORKS OUT HIS PLAN
Genesis 28:13-15

The lives of Abraham, Isaac and Jacob are recorded in the book of Genesis. Now we come to the book of Exodus. From it we learn that the people of Israel were in the land of Egypt instead of in their own country. Why had the Israelites left Canaan and gone to Egypt? (*Teacher:* Refer to map.)

God knew His chosen people would be tempted to live like the wicked Canaanites. So He prepared a special place for them in another land. There they wouldn't get mixed up with the wicked Canaanites. They would learn, instead, to trust God alone.

Since God has all power, He is completely in charge of people and nations. In His plan, God allowed one of Jacob's 12 sons, Joseph, to be taken from Canaan to Egypt. There Joseph became an assistant to Pharaoh the king. Years later God caused a severe famine to come upon Canaan. There was no food for the people. There was none for the animals.

One day Jacob heard news that there was food in Egypt. He called his sons together. "Why do you stand around looking at one another?" he asked. "There is grain in Egypt. (Refer to map on back cover.. Go down there and buy some for us before we all starve to death!" he demanded. (See Genesis 42:1-2.)

His sons obeyed immediately. In Egypt, they had to go to the king's assistant to ask for grain. They didn't recognize this man as their younger brother, Joseph. It had been years since they had seen him. He was dressed in Egyptian clothes. He spoke the Egyptian language. Joseph recognized his brothers and cried when he saw them. But he didn't let them see his tears. Nor did he let them know that he was their brother. He simply commanded his servants to fill their sacks with grain and sent them home.

Show Illustration #4

Later the brothers returned to buy more grain. Then Joseph told them, "I am your brother. You sold me as a slave. But I still love you. *God* sent me here so I could provide for you and your families during the famine. He wants to preserve our people and make us a great nation." (See Genesis 45:7-8.)

Pharaoh, king of Egypt, was pleased when he heard that Joseph's brothers had come. "Joseph," he said, "tell your brothers to go get your father and their families and bring them to Egypt. I will give them some of the good land in Egypt. (See Genesis 45:18; 47:1-6.) They may settle there, take care of their flocks of animals and be safe."

Joseph's father, Jacob, was an old man by this time. It wasn't easy for him to leave his home and go to a new place. But again God came to him during the night. "Jacob," He said, "don't be afraid to go to Egypt. I will go with you. I will make of you and your children a great nation. Someday I will bring your descendants (the Israelites) back to Canaan—the land I promised to your grandfather, Abraham." (See Genesis 46:3-4a.)

Jacob and his sons did not understand all that God was doing. But they believed His promises. They obeyed His commands. They followed His instructions.

As God loved Abraham, Isaac, Jacob and their descendants, so He loves you and me. He has a special plan for each of us, as He did for them. Do you believe that the Lord Jesus Christ is the Son of God? Will you place your trust in Him? Will you ask Him to forgive your sins? God has a wonderful plan for you. He wants to use you–not because you're better than anyone else, but because He can give you power to obey and follow Him. Will you let the Lord take charge of your life?

Lesson 2
GOD CHOOSES A MAN

NOTE TO THE TEACHER

Election is an important Bible doctrine. It may be defined as "The action of God in choosing certain people for certain purposes." (*Teacher:* The information in this note is adapted from a splendid book which you should have. It is entitled, *A Survey of Bible Doctrine* by Dr. Charles C. Ryrie, available from Moody Press, Chicago, IL.)

The people and groups whom God elects vary. For example: (1) God elected Israel as a nation (Deuteronomy 4:37; 1 Chronicles 16:13); (2) God chose King Cyrus, though he was not saved as far as we know (Isaiah 45:1-4); (3) The Lord Jesus Christ is God's elect (Isaiah 42:1); (4) During the tribulation there will be an elect people who are different from the Church (Matthew 24:22, 24, 31); (5) Believers in Christ today are elect of God (Colossians 3:12; Titus 1:1).

Election is not an easy subject. But if we can begin to believe it (even though we may not fully understand), then we are beginning to see election from God's point of view. (See lesson #4 for more on the subject of election.)

Scripture to be studied: Exodus 1:1–2:10; Acts 7:18-22; all verses in the text

The *aim* of the lesson: To show that God chooses nations and people for special purposes so His plan may be fulfilled.

   What your students should *know*: Life includes difficulties, problems, suffering and disappointments which are used together to work out God's will.

   What your students should *feel*: A yearning to live victoriously even in the unfavorable circumstances of life.

   What your students should *do*: Accept their present difficulties triumphantly with complete trust in God, the sovereign One.

Lesson outline (for the teacher's and students' notebooks):

1. The suffering of the people of God (Exodus 1:7-22).
2. What the people of God needed (Exodus 2:24-25; 3:7).
3. The plan of God for His people (Exodus 2:1-10).
4. The protection of God for His chosen one (Exodus 2:1-10).

The verse to be memorized:

Ye have not chosen Me, but I have chosen you. (John 15:16a)

THE LESSON

Have you ever been chosen to do something special? Would you tell us how you felt about that? (Encourage class discussion.) Suppose God Himself chose you for some special purpose. How would that make you feel?

Long, long ago, in the land of Egypt, God chose a baby for a particular reason. Why did God need him? Why was the baby in Egypt? How did the parents of the baby know God had chosen their son? Listen carefully.

Jacob and his twelve sons–a family God had chosen for His own special purposes–were out of their homeland. He had given them the land of Canaan. But they had moved down to Egypt because of a famine. If they hadn't done so, they would have starved to death. Instead of going home when the famine was over, they stayed and they stayed and they stayed (about 400 years!). In time, things changed. Jacob died. His sons died. Pharaoh, the friendly king of Egypt, died. (See Exodus 1:6-8.)

But the descendants of Jacob, the Israelites, kept increasing. They became a large nation (about two million people!) just as God had promised Jacob (Genesis 46:3).

1. THE SUFFERING OF THE PEOPLE OF GOD
Exodus 1:7-22

A new Pharaoh was now the king of Egypt. He was not at all friendly to the Israelites as the other Pharaoh had been. He did not like these people. He saw how fast they were multiplying. He was afraid to have so many foreigners in his land. He thought to himself, *These people are strong! They might give me real trouble.*

Pharaoh called his leaders together. "Have you observed the strength of these Israelites?" he asked. "They might join our enemies and fight against us. We must stop them from multiplying and becoming so strong."

The leaders gave Pharaoh an idea. "You are building big cities and need thousands of bricks. Force the Israelites to make the bricks. They are shepherds. They're not used to this kind of work. If you make them work hard enough, it will probably kill them."

"An excellent idea!" Pharaoh declared. "We will make them slaves. Choose men to be masters over them. Give the masters large whips. Tell them to beat the Israelites and make them work harder. Don't pity them. If they die, good! That will solve our problems!"

The poor Israelites! Year after year they suffered as Pharaoh's orders were obeyed. They dug stiff clay. They kneaded it with their hands and feet. They shaped it in molds, making bricks, bricks and more bricks.

"Oh, the sun is so hot!" one moaned. "My hands are sore!" cried another. "My feet have blisters!" "My back is aching!" So the Israelite men groaned as they slaved hour after hour.

Crack! went the master's whip. And another red welt rose on the aching back.

Pharaoh watched. "They'll get weak now," he laughed. "They'll die before long. Then we will be rid of these people."

Ah, Pharaoh didn't realize that God had chosen the Israelites as His special people. Pharaoh didn't know that he was the one who was on the losing side. For when he fought against the people of God, he was really fighting against God. (See Isaiah 54:17.)

Instead of becoming fewer in number, the Israelites multiplied. Pharaoh and his leaders probably had another meeting. "I cannot believe this!" Pharaoh announced. "The harder these people work, the stronger they become. Are you really lashing them? Do you make them work from morning until night? Punish them more!"

Then Pharaoh thought of another wicked plan. He ordered two women (named Shiphrah and Puah) to come to his palace. These two (known as "midwives") helped the Israelite women when their babies were born.

Pharaoh said to them, "Listen to me! Kill every Israelite baby boy when he is born. Do you understand? This is my command!" (See Exodus 1:16.)

When the midwives left Pharaoh's palace, one exclaimed, "We can't obey his order! We would be murderers! We must *disobey* Pharaoh and *trust* God." That is exactly what they did. And God honored them. (See Exodus 1:20.)

No matter how much Pharaoh made the people suffer, they became stronger. They increased in number because God was blessing His chosen people.

Finally the king of Egypt had another evil plan. He sent a news bulletin throughout the whole land, "This is a command! Throw every Israelite baby boy into the Nile River! All are to be drowned or eaten by the crocodiles!"

Show Illustration #5

The Egyptian soldiers rushed into the Israelites' homes. They grabbed the baby boys from their mothers' arms! The babies screamed in terror. Fathers, mothers, brothers, sisters ran after the soldiers crying and begging them not to kill their babies. But it was hopeless.

Satan, through Pharaoh, was determined to destroy God's people. Today, thousands of years later, he still tries to destroy people. He keeps people from believing that Jesus Christ loves them and died for their sins. (See 2 Corinthians 4:4.) Satan wants them to be separated from God forever. He hates God and His purposes.

2. WHAT THE PEOPLE OF GOD NEEDED
Exodus 2:24-25; 3:7

Show Illustration #6

God saw the soldiers murdering the boy babies. He saw His people fall under the cruel lashings of the Egyptians. He saw the great sadness of His people. He heard their crying. And God cared. (See Exodus 2:23-25; 3:7-8.) Even though they didn't suspect it, He was working out His particular plan for them.

God knew that His people needed a deliverer. They needed a man to lead them out of Egypt, away from the awful murders and slavery of the wicked Pharaoh. God's ways are perfect. (See Psalm 18:30a.) So is His timing. Hundreds of years before this, God had told Abraham, "My people will live in Egypt 400 years. Then they will return to the land of Canaan which I have chosen for them." (See Genesis 15:13-14.) Now the 400 years had passed. It was time for the people of God to go home.

3. THE PLAN OF GOD FOR HIS PEOPLE
Exodus 2:1-10

Although everything seemed impossible, God was at work. First, *He chose a home*–the home of Jochebed and Amram. (See Exodus 6:20.) Into that home he sent a splendid son. Because he was an Israelite, he would be destroyed by Pharaoh's soldiers. Jochebed was terrified. She whispered to her husband, "Amram, I'm not going to let the soldiers drown our baby in the Nile River! I'm going to hide him! Our trust is in God and I refuse to be afraid of the wicked king." (See Hebrews 11:23.)

Amram agreed to help her. Their two older children (Miriam and Aaron) determined to keep the secret and help their parents hide the baby.

Whenever the baby whimpered, someone ran to him, clapped a hand over his mouth, picked him up and kept him quiet.

Show Illustration #7

When Jochebed rocked the little baby, she looked first into his bright eyes, then to Heaven above. "O God," she prayed, "please keep my baby safe. I want him to believe in You, the true and living God. I want him to know that we are Your chosen people. Take us back to our homeland–the land You have chosen for us. Please, dear Lord, help me to hide my baby."

God answered Jochebed's prayer. *He chose to keep this one Israelite baby safe for His special purpose.*

Why did God choose the son of Jochebed and Amram? He doesn't tell us. And we don't need to know. He is all-wise and is in charge of everything. It's not necessary for Him to explain why He acts and chooses as He does. His ways are perfect.

4. THE PROTECTION OF GOD FOR HIS CHOSEN ONE
Exodus 2:1-10

As the baby grew, his voice became stronger. It was more difficult for his family to keep him quiet.

Then one day God gave Jochebed an idea. She made a watertight boat-like basket. Holding her baby close, she hugged him and kissed him. Lovingly she tucked him into the basket. "O God," she prayed, "please protect my baby."

Taking one last loving look, she covered him carefully. She picked up the boat-basket and, with her daughter, stepped outside, looking this way and that. They tiptoed down the road, praying–oh so earnestly!–that the baby wouldn't cry. When they got to the edge of the river, Jochebed placed the basket among the reeds (or bushes). There, she knew Pharaoh's daughter would come to worship the river god and bathe. This was the same river (the Nile) where the baby boys were being put to death. Jochebed trusted God to take care of her baby son right there!

She had done all she could. Silently she turned toward home, leaving her daughter (Miriam) close by, but out of sight. Miriam watched and waited breathlessly.

Soon there was a flurry at the palace. The princess, Pharaoh's daughter, came out to worship and bathe. Seeing the little boat, the princess commanded one of her servants, "Get the basket." As she uncovered it, her mouth fell open. "A baby! A darling baby!" she exclaimed. "This is a child of an Israelite. He is adorable! What a pity it would be to destroy him!" A moment later she added, "We can't do it. No matter what my father has commanded, we can't drown him."

When Miriam saw that the princess cared for her little brother, she slipped from her hiding place. "Would you like me to find an Israelite nurse to take care of the baby for you?" she asked courageously.

"Yes, please do," the princess replied.

Miriam ran home as fast as she could. "Mother! Come quickly!" she exclaimed. "The princess has been kind to our baby. She needs a nurse to care for him. She told me to find one for her. Come with me right now!"

Jochebed raced after Miriam, praying as she went. "Thank You, dear God, for keeping my son safe," she prayed.

At the river, Jochebed bowed low before the princess. Her heart was pounding so wildly, she could hardly hear what the princess was saying.

Show Illustration #8

"Take this child to your home," the princess commanded. "Nurse him and train him. And I will pay you." Imagine that! God arranged for the baby's *own mother* to take care of him.

No longer did Jochebed have to hide her son. No longer did someone have to pick him up each time he made a noise. The whole family could enjoy him. And Pharaoh's own daughter was his protector! Later she (the princess) named him Moses.

God always gives us much more than we ask or even think. (See Ephesians 3:20.) Jochebed had the joy of caring for her baby son, and the princess even *paid* her to do it! Satan expected to destroy *all* the Israelite boys. But God had chosen Moses for Himself and kept him safe for His special purpose. God always carries out His plan in His way, in His time.

He loves you and me just as much as He loved that baby and his family. God loves us so much that He sent His Son, the Lord Jesus Christ, to die on the cross for our sins. (See John 3:16.) Do you believe that Jesus is the Son of God? Do you believe He died for you? If you do, will you ask Him to forgive your sins? Will you receive Him as your Saviour? If you will, He will forgive your sin. Someday you will go to be with Him in Heaven forever.

Until that day, He wants to use you for Himself. I don't know what He wants you to do. But this I know: He has a plan for your life. And if you'll let Him, He'll use you as He has planned. But first He wants you to become a member of His family. You become a member of God's family by placing your trust in His Son. Will you do that right now?

Lesson 3
GOD CHOOSES A LEADER

Scripture to be studied: Exodus 2:9–4:18; Acts 7:20-35

The *aim* of the lesson: To illustrate that God wants to prepare His own so they are able to lead others to believe in the Lord and serve Him.

- **What your students should *know*:** God may use many things–other people, things that happen, what they hear and see, places they live–to mold their lives so He can use them to do His work.
- **What you students should *feel*:** Willing to allow God to work out His purposes in their lives.
- **What your students should *do*:** Ask God to train and equip them, starting this very day, so they will be servants He can use.

Lesson outline (for the teacher's and students' notebooks):
1. The preparation of Moses (Exodus 2:9-11).
2. God's care of Moses (Exodus 2:10; Acts 7:21-22).
3. Moses makes a mistake (Exodus 2:11-25; Acts 7:23-29).
4. The promises of God (Exodus 3:1–4:18; Acts 7:30-35).

The verse to be memorized:

Ye have not chosen Me, but I have chosen you. (John 15:16a)

THE LESSON

Have you ever made something with clay? How did you make it? (*Teacher:* If possible, take some clay to class and shape it while teaching.)

Did you ever watch a potter make bowls or vases or pitchers? He spins the clay and works it with his hands until it is the shape and size he wants. The clay does not tell the potter how it wants to be shaped. The potter has a plan. And he can do with the clay as he pleases.

God wants to shape our lives just as the potter shapes his clay. (See Jeremiah 18:6; Romans 9:21.) God knows what He wants us to be. He knows exactly how He plans to use us. The problem is, we can talk back. Often we refuse to allow God to make us into what He has planned.

1. THE PREPARATION OF MOSES
Exodus 2:9-11

Long ago, God chose Moses for a special purpose. Immediately He began shaping Moses' life. It took many, many years to mold Moses. *We're* usually in a big hurry. But *God* is never in a hurry.

Moses needed spiritual training for the task God had in mind. The daughter of Pharaoh let Jochebed, Moses' mother, take the baby Moses home to nurse him and train him. Certainly Jochebed told Moses about the living God who loved him and saved his life. She told him about God's commanding Abraham (hundreds of years before) to leave his home, his family, and his friends. She told him of Abraham's obedience and God's leading him to Canaan.

"And, Moses, Canaan is our homeland. That is where God wants our people to live," she told him over and over. "We are slaves of the Egyptians now. God told our father Abraham we would live here in Egypt for 400 years. When that time is over, we will go back to our homeland.

"Soon you must go to the palace to live with the princess. Don't be afraid. We'll pray for you. Always remember the miraculous way God has cared for you, Moses. Surely He will use you in a special way."

In this little home and through a godly mother, God began to shape the young boy.

Moses often saw his mother crying because his father was treated cruelly. He watched the Israelite men come home each night. All had big welts on their backs–welts from the whips of the Egyptians. He saw how sad they were.

Also *Moses needed royal training* for the task God had in mind.

The day came when Jochebed had to take her boy to his new home. She held him close and prayed, "Dear God, please take care of Moses. Help him to remember that You have chosen us Israelites for Yourself. May he love and serve You always. Never let him worship the Egyptian idols." Turning, she led her boy to the palace and to his adoptive mother, the princess.

How life changed for Moses! Instead of being the son of a slave, he was now a grandson of the king! He was a prince! He wore only the finest clothes. He ate the best foods. When he rode through the streets, everyone bowed before him. When he went boating on the Nile River, he used the golden royal barge. Many servants took care of him and did whatever he asked.

Show Illustration #9

But something else changed too. He no longer heard anything about the true and living God of Heaven. Instead, his adoptive mother, the princess, worshiped gods of stone and marble. These gods had eyes that could not see and ears that could not hear. (See Psalm 115:5-7.)

For the task God had in mind, *Moses needed training in the Egyptian schools and universities.*

Moses attended the best schools in Egypt. He learned the great wisdom of the Egyptians. (See Acts 7:22.)

2. GOD'S CARE OF MOSES
Exodus 2:10; Acts 7:21-22

Think of it! Moses, an Israelite, was being trained and cared for in the home of the very one who wanted to destroy the Israelites. Remember, God is all-wise. He is over everything and has a plan for each one. He was shaping Moses into a man who could lead others. And the palace was the one place he could get the necessary training.

Show Illustration #10

When Moses became a young man, he led the Egyptian army when they went out to fight. Pharaoh thought, *What a fine captain Moses is! Our Egyptian army always wins when he leads them.* But Moses thought, *Oh, how my own people are suffering! If only I could lead them out of slavery.*

As a member of the king's family, Moses learned to speak well before many important people. (See Acts 7:22.) But Moses could never forget his own mother, his father, his sister (Miriam) and his brother (Aaron). He could never forget the cruel treatment they and the other Israelite slaves received. He thought of the day when the children of Israel would return to their homeland, Canaan–the land God had promised them.

Year after year went by. Moses was almost 40 years old. And God was still preparing him.

3. MOSES MAKES A MISTAKE
Exodus 2:11-25; Acts 7:23-29

Moses needed training to learn how to depend on God.

One day as Moses watched his countrymen making bricks, he thought, *How tired they look! How unhappy they are! How hard they are working!*

Crack! went the Egyptian's whip on the back of an Israelite.

"What right does that Egyptian have to beat my people?" Moses exclaimed. "I'll teach him a lesson!"

Show Illustration #11

Moses looked this way and that. No one was watching. Wham! He knocked the Egyptian to the ground. What a blow! The Egyptian lay dead. Quickly Moses covered him with sand and went his way.

The next day Moses went again to see how things were going among the Israelites. He was certain now that God wanted him to make their lives easier. But he failed to ask God for guidance.

This day, he saw two Israelite men fighting each other. "Why are you hitting an Israelite brother?" he asked.

One replied angrily, "Who made you our master? Are you going to kill me as you killed that Egyptian?"

Moses was terrified. He knew he had done wrong. He had no right to murder anyone.

When Pharaoh heard the news he was furious. "Moses will die for this!" he shouted.

What should Moses do? He was confused and disturbed. He wasn't really afraid of the king. (See Hebrews 11:27.) For he felt certain that God wanted him to deliver his people out of slavery. But why didn't they welcome him as their deliverer? He had to find the answer for himself. So he left Egypt. But where should he go?

Moses wandered on and on. After many days, he came to the land of Midian. Midian was a land of shepherds (people who had large flocks of animals). When Moses got to Midian he sat down by a well to rest. Just at that time seven girls came to the well with their flocks of sheep. As usual, some rough, rude shepherds pushed the girls aside so their own sheep could drink first.

When Moses saw what happened, he grabbed the rude men and shoved them out of the way. The quivering shepherds stood back and waited while the girls watered their sheep first.

When the girls got home, their father, Reuel, exclaimed, "You're home early today! What happened?"

The girls all talked at once. "An Egyptian was by the well. When the shepherds pushed in ahead of us as they always do, he forced them aside so our sheep could drink first."

"Where is he?" asked their father. "Go back immediately and ask him to eat with us."

Moses gladly accepted their invitation, ate supper and spent the night. So it was that Moses lived with Reuel and his family. He cared for Reuel's flocks.

What a contrast from life in the palace! Day after day he sat on the hillside while the sheep grazed. All he heard was the baaing of sheep. How quiet his life had become! Moses thought and thought. He was a good shepherd. He was loved and respected by Reuel.

The day came when Moses and Zipporah, one of Reuel's daughters, were married. In the years that followed, Moses and Zipporah had two little boys.

Forty years went by. Moses was 80 years old. God is never in a hurry. He had trained Moses in Egypt for 40 busy years in the palace. He kept him in the quiet life of Midian as a shepherd for 40 years. Here Moses had plenty of time to think.

4. THE PROMISES OF GOD
Exodus 3:1–4:18; Acts 7:30-35

Show Illustration #12

One day while Moses was tending his sheep, he saw a bush on fire. But the bush didn't burn up!

"Moses, Moses!" a voice called from the flaming bush.

Startled, Moses replied, "Here I am."

The voice commanded, "Don't come any closer. Take off your shoes. You are standing on holy ground. I am God–the One who spoke to Abraham, to Isaac and to Jacob."

God continued, "The time has come for Me to help your people, the Israelites, in Egypt. I have seen their misery. They have cried to Me and I have heard them. I am going to deliver them out of Egypt. You will be the one to lead them. Go to the king of Egypt. Tell him this: 'God has commanded me (Moses) to lead the Israelites out of Egypt.'"

"O God," he answered, "who am I that You want to send me? I couldn't do anything like that." Forty years of sheep-herding had changed Moses. He was no longer a self-confident young man.

"Do not worry, Moses," God assured him. "I will be with you."

"But, God, when the Israelites ask who sent me, what will I say to them?"

"Simply tell them that Jehovah–the God of their fathers Abraham, Isaac and Jacob–has sent you."

"But, God, they won't believe me. They will never do what I say."

"Moses, take your shepherd's rod which you have in your hand. Throw it on the ground," God commanded.

Moses obeyed. To his surprise the rod turned into a snake.

"Pick it up by the tail, Moses!" God ordered. The snake became a rod again.

"Moses, put your hand on your chest inside your robe."

Moses obeyed. When he pulled his hand out it was covered with a dread disease, leprosy.

"Now put it in again, Moses." When he pulled it out, it was all well.

"Moses, when you show these signs to the children of Israel, they'll know that I sent you."

"But, God, I cannot speak."

"Moses, I will put into your mouth the words I want you to speak. You do not need to worry. Just be willing to lead My people for Me. I will do the rest."

But Moses argued, "I don't want to go alone."

How patient and long-suffering God was as He dealt with Moses! Instead of giving up and choosing someone else, God promised to send Moses' brother, Aaron, with him to do the speaking for him.

Finally, Moses told God he was willing to go and do whatever God commanded. What a different Moses! He was at last the kind of man God would be able to use. Instead of using his own wisdom and acting in his own strength, Moses was now ready to depend upon God completely. God had used the experiences of life to mold and shape Moses for His use.

Do you ask God for His guidance, then follow it? Or do you do what you yourself choose? Are you going your own way? Are you willing to ask Him today to shape your life as He wills? He wants to do that. And He will do it, if you allow Him to.

Lesson 4
GOD'S CHOICE TODAY

NOTE TO THE TEACHER

Like everything God does, election totally agrees with His character. For example: (1) Election is loving, for God is love (see Ephesians 1:4-5); (2) Election is wise, because God is wise (Jude 25); (3) Election began in eternity past (Ephesians 1:4); it extends throughout eternity future (Romans 8:30); (4) Election glorifies God (Ephesians 1:12-14).

This may be difficult for us to understand. But we see only a small part of all that God is doing. So we cannot know His entire plan.

Doing good works is a product of election. (See Ephesians 2:10.) The elect of God are to be merciful, kind, humble, meek, long-suffering. (See Colossians 3:12.)

In seeking to grasp why God sovereignly elects (or chooses), our attitude should be one of amazement and gratitude. (See Romans 11:33-36.)

These notes, like those in lesson #2, are adapted from Dr. Ryrie's excellent book, *A Survey of Bible Doctrine*. We have not included the information dealing with election and salvation, since that is outside the scope of this series of lessons.

Teach the memory verse with awe. Christ bought us at a tremendous price (1 Peter 1:18-20). Yet we did not choose to serve Him. He chose us. Think of that!

Scripture to be studied: Ephesians 1; Romans 3; all verses in text.

The *aim* of the lesson: To show the wonderful privilege of being chosen to know and serve God, the all-wise, all-powerful, all-knowing One.

What your students should *know*: That God has always worked according to His own wonderful plan. He has the right to direct their lives.

What your students should *feel*: Gratitude to God for choosing them for Himself and a desire to fulfill His plan for their lives.

What your students should *do*: Take definite steps toward finding God's plan for their lives.

Lesson outline (for the teacher's and students' notebooks):

1. God chooses the places He puts us.
2. God chooses the privileges He gives us.
3. God chooses the people He brings into our lives.
4. God chooses a plan for our lives.

The verse to be memorized:

Ye have not chosen Me, but I have chosen you. (John 15:16a)

THE LESSON

Things don't just happen. The God of the universe, the Creator of the world, has planned everything. And all things take place according to His marvelous plan. He is all-wise and all-powerful. He has all ability and He is in command. He was in command long ago when Abraham and Moses lived. He is *still* in command. He cares about nations and leaders and important people. And He cares about you and me. (See 1 Peter 5:7.)

1. GOD CHOOSES THE PLACES HE PUTS US

God in His wisdom and His greatness chooses the very PLACES in which He puts us. He allowed Joseph to be taken from his homeland–Canaan–to Egypt. There Joseph would be able to provide for his family when, years later, they came needing food.

God led Joseph's family–the Israelites–out of Canaan and into Egypt so they would grow into a nation. He wanted them to be a special people for Himself. From the very beginning, He planned to send His only Son, the Lord Jesus Christ, to the world. He would send Him through this nation.

Show Illustration #13

(*Teacher:* Point to appropriate part of illustration as students discuss the following three paragraphs.)

In what kind of family did God put Moses? *(He gave Moses a mother and father who believed in the living God of Heaven. They taught Moses about God and His plans for the Israelites.)*

According to God's plan, where did Moses get his education and training? *(In the palace)* Why did God choose the palace for Moses? *(It was there he could receive the training he needed to become a successful leader.)*

After all this education, Moses had to learn to depend on *God* rather than upon his own strength. So God sent him to Midian. There he worked as a shepherd. And there he learned that God alone was his strength.

God often changes our location in order to shape us into the kind of person He has planned.

God chose the family into which He put you. This didn't just happen. He put you into this very neighborhood where you could come to class and hear His Word. Everything that happens to you each day is planned by God. He wants to shape you into the kind of person He wants you to become. (See Ephesians 1:11-12.)

2. GOD CHOOSES THE PRIVILEGES HE GIVES US

In His wisdom and goodness God chooses the PRIVILEGES He gives us.

1. What a privilege for Abraham, Isaac, Jacob and Moses to KNOW God! He appeared to them. He spoke to them. He helped them to understand what He is like and what He wanted them to do.

These men of long ago are not the only ones to have the privilege of knowing God. You, too, have that privilege. Today we have His Holy Word, the Bible. In this, His Book, God tells us what He is like. Through His Word He helps us know who He is and what He wants us to be and do.

See Illustration #14

If we want to learn about God and His Son, the Lord Jesus Christ, we must read the Bible. We must study His Word. One of the many truths we learn from the Bible is the importance of prayer.

2. Prayer is a privilege. The Israelites used their privilege of PRAYING to God. When they were cruelly treated in Egypt, they cried, "O Lord, have mercy upon us. Please take us out of Egypt."

Jochebed, an Israelite mother, used her privilege of prayer. "Dear God," she began, "please watch over my little baby in this boat-basket. Don't let him drown. I don't know how You can save him. But I believe You will. Thank You, dear heavenly Father."

God heard and answered the prayer of the Israelites. He heard and answered Jochebed's prayer. He is the same today (Hebrews 13:8). He hears and answers us when we pray (Jeremiah 33:3). To us, God says in His Word, "Do not worry about anything. Pray to me about everything." (See Philippians 4:6.)

It is our privilege to PRAY to the true and living God! He cares about us. He knows all our needs. He wants to answer our prayers.

3. Protection is a privilege. God protected Jochebed's baby when she put him in the basket at the river's edge. Almighty God, the Creator, watched over that tiny baby in order to accomplish His wonderful plan.

Satan wanted to spoil God's plan. So he used Pharaoh to try to destroy the Israelites. What did Pharaoh do? (*Teacher:* Review his efforts as found in lesson #2.) Satan would have been delighted to destroy all the Israelites including Moses. He wanted to ruin God's plan. But God is all-powerful. He protected His people. He wouldn't allow them to be wiped out. It is a glorious privilege to be protected by Almighty God Himself.

Did you know that we who have trusted the Lord Jesus Christ as our Saviour are held in God's hand? (*Teacher:* Point to person in hands in illustration #14.) The Lord Jesus said that those who trust in Him have eternal life. They will never perish. He said, "Neither shall any man pluck them out of my hand." You are held right *in the Saviour's hand.* Then as if that were not enough, He says that no man is able to pluck believers out of *His Father's hand.* (Cup one hand over the other to demonstrate the security of being protected by the Father and Son.). What a privilege to be PROTECTED in that place which even Satan cannot touch!

Satan knows this, too. He cannot pluck us out of the Father's hand. But he *can* cause us to disobey God. Satan is delighted when we lie, steal, hate or get angry. By ourselves, we do these things. But when our trust is in Christ, He rescues us by the power of the Holy Spirit who lives in us–right in our hearts. (See 1 Corinthians 6:19; Galatians 2:20.)

At the beginning of each new day, it is good to talk to God about this. Your prayer could include: "Lord, by myself I cannot live the way You want me to live today. But I thank You that Your Holy Spirit is willing to help me. I want to obey You and please You in all that I do."

The Holy Spirit can protect you from a life of sin. Then you will be free to serve the living God as He has planned.

3. GOD CHOOSES THE PEOPLE HE BRINGS INTO OUR LIVES

Our lives are affected by people. So God uses PEOPLE to shape us for His plan and purpose.

Pharaoh ordered the midwives in Israel to destroy the baby boys. But God showed them this was wrong. He gave them the courage to disobey Pharaoh. He used them to protect the babies.

God used Pharaoh's daughter for His purpose. She provided protection and the best education and training for Moses. Did this just happen? No, everything was against such a possibility. But "with God, nothing shall be impossible" (Luke 1:37).

Teachers, pastors, friends and relatives all help to mold our lives. How important it is to listen to those who love the Lord and believe His Word! We become like our friends. Have you chosen friends who love the Saviour? (See 1 Corinthians 15:33.)

Show Illustration #15

Do *you* love the Saviour? God loves you. He gave His Son, the Lord Jesus Christ, to die on the cross for your sins. He wants to give you eternal life. All are sinners (Romans 3:23). No one is good (Romans 3:10). But God loves you even though you have sinned. (See Romans 5:8.)

God has chosen you to hear this message of His love. He led you to this class *today*. He wants you to know that the Lord Jesus died for your sins. He wants to give you eternal life. To have the gift of eternal life means that you will live forever and ever with God in Heaven. But you can have this gift only by receiving the Lord Jesus as your Saviour.

What are you going to do about it? You must make a decision. Do you believe that Jesus Christ is the Son of God? Do you believe He died for you? Will you place all your trust in Him? He is God's gift of love to you. Will you receive Him? (*Teacher:* Point to figure accepting the Saviour.)

Because of God's great love for you He gave His Son to die for you. (See John 3:16.) But God loves His Son so much that He will not allow anyone who rejects Him to enter Heaven. (See John 3:36.) (*Teacher:* Point to figure rejecting Christ.)

Will you trust the Lord Jesus to forgive your sins?

4. GOD CHOOSES A PLAN FOR OUR LIVES

God, Who is all-wise, chooses a PLAN for each life. God had a plan for Abraham. He asked Abraham to leave his home and go to a new country. Abraham did not reply, "But God, I like it here. I don't want to go anywhere else." Instead, Abraham knew that God's ways are best. And he did exactly what God had asked him to. God blessed Abraham, gave him great wealth and made him the father of a great nation.

God had a plan for Moses. One day he told Moses' mother, Jochebed, to give her little boy to the princess. She didn't answer, "No, God, I love him too much to let him live in that wicked palace. I don't believe You can take care of him there." She had taught Moses to trust God and obey Him. She had helped him to understand that it always pays to follow God's leading. Many years later, Moses could have had a high position and the wealth of Egypt. Instead, he chose to leave Egypt and suffer along with his own people, the Israelites, as God had planned. (See Hebrews 11:24-26.)

For Abraham and Moses, to obey God may have seemed more difficult than doing what they themselves wanted to do. God's ways are not our ways. (See Isaiah 55:8-9.) But His way is perfect. (See Psalm 18:30.)

Show Illustration #16

God has a PLAN for your life. As you study His Word, He will teach it to you.

His plan, first of all, is for you to be a member of His family. When you place all your trust in the Lord Jesus Christ, God's Son, you become a member of the family of God.

If you are a child of God, the Lord Jesus says to you as He said long ago, "You have not chosen Me, but I have chosen you . . . ." And He has chosen you to do certain things for Him. I cannot know why He has chosen you. I cannot know what He wants you to do. But He has a plan for your life. Think for a few minutes about that plan. Write it in your notebook.

The PLACES God has chosen for me.
The PRIVILEGES God has given to me.
The PEOPLE God has brought into my life.

God has put you into your home, in your neighborhood and in this class for some special purpose. How has He been shaping you for Himself in these places? List in your notebook the privileges God has given to you. You have the glorious privilege of knowing God, of studying His Word, of praying. If you are His child, you have His protection. (Show Illustration #14.) What other privileges do you have? Will you list those in your notebook?

God has brought many people into your life. List in your notebook those who have been helpful to you.

As God talked to Abraham and Moses in the long, long ago, so He wants to talk to you today. His way of talking to His own now is to speak to them through His Word, the Bible. He says "I will instruct you and teach you in the way that you should go: I will guide you with My eye" (Psalm 32:8). His Word, He says is a lamp to your feet and a light to your path (Psalm 119:105). If you will let Him have His way, He will direct your paths. (See Proverbs 3:6.)

List in your notebook some things you can do to let God have His way in your life.

Do you think you know what God wants to do with your life? If so, write that in your notebook. How can you be prepared for His purpose? (*Teacher:* If possible, pray for each one by name. Commit them to the Lord, asking for His plan for each life.)

www.ingramcontent.com/pod-product-compliance
Lightning Source LLC
Chambersburg PA
CBHW060801090426
42736CB00002B/112